TAKING THE BULLY BY THE HORNS

By **Kathy Noll** with **Dr. Jay Carter**

www.hometown.aol.com/Kthynoll

♥ Kathy Noll

Dedicated to anyone who's ever been bullied.

TABLE OF CONTENTS

Acknowledgments

Many thanks to the following people for their help with the book:

Jay Carter, who encouraged me to write the book, Helen Hoover, my instructor from the Children's Institute of Literature in Conn., Thom Keller, Fonzie Jones, George Seidel, Jason Butko, & Jim Wendel for their computer knowledge, and the many friends, family members, and teachers who helped as readers, and shared their own "bully" stories with me: Ed Keim, David, Mary Ann, Melissa, and Paul Kershner, Mary Noll, Jennifer Noll, Betty Smith, Robby Tobias, and Ashley Brobst.

In Loving Memory of my Dear Dad,
Elmer W. Noll,
and all the times he got picked on for his name!

From The Author:

Dear Reader,

Did you know that we've all been bullied at some time in our lives--whether we liked it or not? Sometimes the bully is so-o sneaky about it that we don't even realize what he's doing to us.

Jay Carter wrote a book called Nasty People for adults because they get bullied too. He asked me to write this book for kids so you can learn how to deal with bullies early in life. So, I'm writing this book for you.

Let me tell you a story about a friend named Greg that I use to hang out with when I was a kid. Greg was the type of tough guy who would go around telling everyone he could eat bricks. And we believed him! Because he had a big voice. We didn't dare question him about it. He bullied us into believing him.

One time, Greg told one of our younger friends to wet his pants, or else. This may sound funny, but the poor kid was scared, so he did it! His mom yelled at him when he came home to change his pants and he told her that Greg made him do it.

"But nobody can <u>make</u> you do anything," she answered. And she was right. He <u>let</u> Greg bully him. He was bullied by the best. We all have been bullied in some way.

I remember another time, when I was in third grade, I had a teacher named Mrs. Perch, who was a real goof. She would kick her foot out behind her when she wrote on the blackboard and flirt with all the boys in the class. Sometimes she even sprayed them with her perfume. I don't know why they let her do that!

One day, she made me stand up in front of the entire class. She told me that I have cats' eyes and they make me look sneaky. Was she just jealous and felt the need to put me down?

First of all, I couldn't change my eyes--even if I wanted to.

TAKING THE BULLY BY THE HORNS

Plus, I like my eyes the way they are. Secondly, in a teacher-student relationship, that was really none of her business. But, out of respect, and not having a response planned, I said nothing back.

If that wasn't bad enough, in seventh grade I sat in back of a girl named Andrea. Andrea always wore more makeup than anybody else. Plus her mom was always buying her the latest fashions in clothes. She even got her a new nose (nose job)! Andrea walked around like she thought she was a model or something. She definitely felt she was cooler than the rest of us.

She and her bully gang (sometimes they attack in numbers) came up to me one time, took off my glasses, and pulled on my eye lashes! They thought my lashes were fake because they were long and dark. They pulled until some came out--then they finally realized they were real. Andrea would pull my glasses off a lot and tell me, "You look so-o pretty without your glasses, you should get contacts." This may sound like a nice compliment--at first. But done enough times by this type of person, it's called bullying. Because she was bossy, she always had to be telling everyone what to do. Bullies like to control you; it's what they do best. They are insecure and have to feel like they're in control.

That's why it was important for me to write this book for you--so you don't grow up feeling bad about yourself or anything you've done that others have made you feel bad about.

When you're younger, it's important to understand the difference between people who really care about you, and nasty people. Your mind is like a sponge now, soaking up everything around you as you learn and grow. But, be careful not to soak up too much from the wrong people, or that sponge could turn into a moldy dish rag!

Your Friend,
Kathy Noll

SO WHAT'S THIS BOOK ABOUT ANYWAY?

This book is about:
1. Bullies.
2. Kids who are being bullied.
3. Kids who feel bad, but don't know why.
4. Discovering why people act like bullies.
5. Ideas on what we can do about stopping it.

Bullying can make you feel:
1. You're a bad person.
2. You're not good enough.
3. Totally unhappy.
4. Scared.
5. Angry!

Hopefully, this book will help. You see, bullying happens in all places, all over the world, at all times. It's happening right now--and we need to stop it! Maybe we won't be able to stop all the bullies, but we can stop the ones that you have to deal with.

A lot of kids and adults go around bullying people and they don't even realize it. Maybe they grew up with bullies and learned to act like them. Yes, even friends and family members can be bullies. And, of course, their job as "the bully" is to make you feel bad, or about as small as the dot at the end of this sentence.

Bullies bully because we let them get away with it, and they know that. When we do this, we give them more power. They're like helium balloons that have to keep sucking up more air until they get big enough to explode in your face. If we wouldn't let ourselves be bullied, bullies wouldn't exist. It's time to pop their balloons!

Now, don't feel bad while reading this book. I wrote it so you stop feeling bad about yourself and do something about it. If you think you are a bully or have ever acted like one, then maybe this book will help you to understand why you do it and how to stop.

Cry if you feel sad, or punch your pillow if you feel angry. Don't hold your feeling inside--and don't blame yourself. It's up to you. Do you want to be happy or not? You <u>do</u> want to be happy, you say? Then, stop letting this happen! I'll show you how.

Hopefully, by the end of this book you'll find yourself thinking, "She's right, I've known this all along," or "That's it! Now I know what to do."

Now let's attack the problem of bullies!

1
THE BULLY

Meeting Your Bullies

How many bullies can you name right now? Even if you can't think of any names, it's possible that somebody could be bullying you and you don't even know it.

Has anyone ever made you feel so-o bad about yourself that you developed a hard outer shell or tough skin? First you start believing you're a bad kid because that's what you were told, then you start acting like one. Guess what? Now, you've become the bully. You've turned into a bully so that you can't be hurt by one--ever again. Or so you think.

You might start talking and acting like a tough guy (or girl), but inside you're helpless and scared. You know this. You're not really a bully; it's just a character you're playing so you can't be bullied anymore. You want to win this time. But, you can't win by doing this because you can't really like yourself like this. Anyway, someone else will take the role, like you did, and it will get passed on and on until there's a ton of bullies ruling the earth and everyone will be miserable! This is called the "Bully Cycle."

Description of a Bully

How do you recognize a bully? Good question! But the answer is "You don't always know." Some bullies are extremely easy to recognize, while the rest are too sneaky to tell--at first! You see, a bully doesn't physically look any different. It's his actions that give him his title. He knows so-o many different ways he can bully you. If there's something you're proud of, he might make fun of it. If there's something that means a lot to you, he might break it. He may even lie and tell you it was an accident.

The sneaky bully will get you when you least expect it. He

might pretend to like the same things you do, then make fun of you later for liking those same things. And he loves doing this in front of your other friends too! He'll keep doing this until he has made you look small. After he can see how rotten he's made you feel, he thinks he has control over you. You're nothing but a robot to him--with buttons he can push to make you feel bad anytime he wants. But, most of the time he feels worse than you. When he's not in control, he's scared. He's afraid of being bullied--maybe from a bully in his past. (Bully Cycle again)

If he thinks you're on to his game, he might stop bullying you for awhile. Soon he's acting as if you're his "good buddy." But don't breathe that sigh of relief just yet. He's actually waiting for you to forget about all the crappy stuff he did to you. That's when he'll catch you off guard and start bullying all over again when you least expect it. It's possible that he was waiting for the right time to beat you out for some sport team or class president. When all along, you thought he was being your friend and supporting you. It's hard to fix this type of bully. They are too sneaky and you can't trust them.

Did you know that a bully acts big, but actually feels pretty small inside? That's why he tries to make you feel bad. He wants you to feel as small as him because he's afraid that you're actually a bigger (meaning "better") person than him. It's really sad if you think about it. The poor guy (or girl).

Maybe he really does want to be your friend but only as long as he can control you. If you accuse him of controlling you, he might get angry and try to make you look like a fool in front of your other friends. He'll tell them that you're a bully because you're accusing him of things. Now, he has you feeling bad again. He's won that round and once again he's in control of you.

Is there something about yourself you don't like? Maybe you're not as tall as you wish you were or your grades haven't been as great as you'd like them to be? If a bully knows these secrets, he'll try to make you feel worse about them. A <u>real</u> friend wouldn't do that. But remember, the bully <u>needs</u> to crush you so he doesn't feel so small. And when you let him do this, you're helping to feed his power. It's not nice what he does, but you can learn how to understand it.

Knowing all this--<u>now</u> how many bullies can you name? Probably more than you can count on both hands--and feet. And your friend's hands and feet for that matter! Even if you had fingers and toes all over your entire body, there wouldn't be enough to count all the bullies you'll meet in your lifetime. Plus, you'd look pretty silly.

The Mean Bully

This person claims to be your "good buddy." Most of the time, he seems as if he really <u>is</u> your pal. However, he also puts you down a lot. And when you try to tell him you don't like that, he acts hurt or offended. "I'd never put down my best buddy," he whines. "How could you think that?"

Sometimes he even talks about you behind your back. Is he secretly jealous of you? Probably, but he'd never admit it.

He might compliment you a lot, then immediately tell you a bunch of lies about all the bad stuff everyone is thinking of you. He's actually very insecure and enjoys telling you <u>bad</u> stuff about yourself to boost his own ego. He needs to feel bigger (better) than you.

The Meaner Bully

She will always make a big fuss about something you've done wrong. She points out every little mistake you make, to try to make you feel as little as those mistakes. (Try saying that sentence 10 times!) She remembers everything you got in trouble for. (And probably has it written down!) She uses all these negative things about you to make you look bad in front of your friends, or anyone who's foolish enough to listen to her.

She knows she's won when she has you agreeing with her that you're really horrible, bad, stupid... If you try to bring up something good about yourself, she'll turn it around somehow. She only cares about two things: Herself--and being in control of you.

The Meanest Bully!

Stay far away from this one! He's out of control most of the time, and might seem sort of crazy. He obviously has a lot of problems built up inside of him and could explode with anger at any minute. If he isn't acting violent, he's probably throwing verbal threats at you. He'll try to take your things, and if you don't give them up, he'll hold a  fist up to you, or tell you how he's gonna physically hurt you.

He might even spit in your face, just for looking at him! You can't figure this type of guy out. Because of all his problems, he doesn't feel good about himself at all. And he doesn't care if everyone hates him or not. It's a shame--he really needs help. Maybe you could tell a parent or his teachers, but tell them not to give your name. (Anonymous tip) The bully might know he really needs help, but still want to bite your head off for interfering.

Be very careful.

Is Anybody Really a Bully?

What is she talking about? (You might be thinking) Of

The Bully

course there are bullies! Isn't this what we've been talking about the whole time? Well, yes and no. First of all, we need to try to believe that everyone has at least some good inside of them. Secondly, as we said before, "the bully" is only a character somebody plays. It's only an "act." You and I may have done a little bullying from time to time, but does that make us "bullies?" It is possible that everyone has played the bully at least once. You'll see when we talk more about the many different games that bullies play. Some are more obvious and down right mean, while others are so-o smooth, you're not even sure how they got you feeling so bad.

You need to know when somebody is bullying you, so you can make it stop <u>before</u> you get hurt. Take notice of anyone who is constantly calling you names, taking your stuff, or making fun of you. Now it's time to check their neck. That's right, you're looking for the zipper to that rubber costume they slip into whenever they need to play "the bully." But, remember, it's only a role-playing game. Try unzipping that bully (not really!) and see if you can see an actual friend peeking out from inside. Maybe this person really does need a friend, or help from the school guidance counselor. If you feel he's worth a friendship, then maybe give him a pat on the back and let him know he's "OK." (Remember, the bully feels pretty small inside.) Or you might say, "I'm going to forget about what you did to me (let it pass), because I like you." But, if he's so nasty that he threatens you or explodes with anger, you're probably better off staying away from him.

Unfortunately, from time to time, people will slip into their bully costumes and hurt you or someone else for no other reason except to make themselves feel better. Again, this could be from hurt <u>they've</u> experienced in their past. Now, they feel they have to take it out on somebody, and you just happen to be in their path. You haven't actually done anything wrong. Always keep in mind that <u>they</u> have the problem and <u>you're OK</u>.

2
THE BULLY GAMES

These are definitely games you <u>don't</u> want to play. As you know, bullies can be boys or girls, men or women, old or young, short or tall, fat or thin--they can even be your teachers, friends, or family... No matter who, one thing for sure is that their games won't be any fun for you.

Trust your feelings as you read this book so you can better understand people when they act mean towards you. Read it with a smile and keep in mind that there are many different types of bullies in the world and they all have different reasons (excuses) for doing it. The minute you start to figure them out, do you know what happens? They find someone else to pick on--maybe a friend of yours. That's when you tell all your friends what you've learned from this book, or you could suggest that they read it themselves.

Everybody is different, so at the end of this book I'll give you a few of my own examples that may help you. But you can learn to handle bullying <u>your </u>way. First let's break down the many different games bullies play.

The Guessing Game

The "Guessing Game" is one way a bully might try to <u>get you</u>. She won't give you a straight answer. Your head will be spinning while she's trying to drive you nuts! She'll have you totally confused about yourself and your environment. You might not know the difference between "up" or "down" by the time she's done with you. And there's lots of

ways she can play this game.

For example, all of sudden she's telling you how much she loves your hair. Then, she'll start buying you snacks or sharing her lunch with you. Now wait a minute--before this girl rarely talked to you--now she's your best friend? Then, after she knows she has your trust, she sinks her teeth into you (hopefully not for real!) She'll now tell you how dirty your hair looks and ask you if you ever wash it. She might even <u>take</u> your lunch just because she "felt like it." She's treating you like a stinking sock!

"What happened?" You ask. "I thought we were friends."

"Of course we're friends," she answers mockingly. "What's your problem?"

Here's where she gets you confused. She wants to know what <u>your</u> problem is. <u>She</u> is the one with the problem but she's passing the buck to you--trying to make you take the blame for all of <u>her</u> problems. When you try to explain to her how she's been making you feel, she swings her hair over her shoulder, and says "I don't know what you're talking about. You're nuts!" Then stomps out the door. You can bet she won't talk to you for awhile, but she'll come back, and she'll be wearing her "best friend" costume again.

Watch out! She has you playing the guessing game as to whether she's "the bully" or "the friend." She'll keep switching back and forth--and soon--you're so confused, she has you wondering if maybe you <u>are</u> the one with the problem. (But we know you're not!)

I Blame <u>You</u>

This is one of the bullies favorite games. He wants to blame you for all the bad junk that's happened to him. For example, he'll tell you that <u>you</u> don't want to be friends with <u>him.</u> The truth is that <u>he</u> doesn't want to be friends with <u>you</u>.

The Bully Games

His statement gets you wondering if you've been acting friendly enough. But don't take it personally. He's the real rat, and now he's laughing to himself because he has you blaming yourself for the rotten things <u>he's</u> doing. If you've ever heard of the word "irony," that's what is happening here.

Sometimes, when somebody is guilty of something, he'll try to blame you for the thing <u>he</u> did wrong. DON'T FALL FOR THIS TRICK! For example, you might start to notice that some of your lunch money has been missing from your desk or jacket pocket. Before you get a chance to ask "the bully" about it, he starts blaming you for stealing <u>his</u> lunch money. Coincidence? No, he beat you to the punch.

Be careful, these bullies are tricky. They know how to turn any situation around to save their own butt. Be aware of this game and always watch your back.

Missing the Point

Look out for this one. This game can make you feel <u>extremely</u> bad about yourself. The rules to this game are as follows: You make a simple mistake, and you get blamed for destroying the Earth. Here's your example: It was your turn to do the dishes after dinner. Everyone in your family takes turns doing the chores. However, you didn't realize it  was your turn because you were busy in your bedroom working on your science project. Minutes later (Boom!), your older sister kicks open the door to your room with the power of an exploding bomb.

"Nice going knuckle-head, because you were upstairs,

TAKING THE BULLY BY THE HORNS

Mom made me do the dishes--and it was your turn. You are so-o stupid, what a little dork!"

This is called a "generalization." The point is that you accidentally forgot it was your turn to do the dishes, not that you're stupid. If you were a genius, it still wouldn't have gotten the dishes done. The important thing is correcting the problem, not name-calling. A simple reminder would have been good enough. The problem is dirty dishes, and getting them clean before raccoons break into the house and lick them clean. Attack the problem, not the person.

Let's take another example where the point is missed by a mile: Mom buys you a new coat because the hand-me-down from your sister doesn't fit anymore. You wear your new coat to school, not even really thinking about it. From down the hall, you hear "the bully" holler up to you, "What a brat!"

Your mind races to think of what you might have done. As she gets closer, you see the smirk on her face as she says, "Look at the brat's new coat. Are you gonna wear a different new coat every week now?" She's beating around the bush. The problem isn't that you're a brat or that you have a new coat; the problem is that she is jealous of you! And that is her problem. In this game, bullies need to stick to the point or shut up!

Judging You Unfairly

Let's go back to the story of your sister calling you "stupid." Name-calling is one of the many weapons of the bully. If she wanted to use an even bigger weapon, she would have said, "<u>Everyone</u> knows you're stupid." If she says this to you enough times, you might start to believe it. Then you'll either feel horrible, or you might even start acting stupid (because that's what everyone thinks anyway, right?) But who is <u>everyone</u>? And how does <u>she</u> know they all think this? Could it be logical that <u>all</u> the people who care about you would tell your sister such a thing? Can you imagine everyone calling her on the phone and lining up to tell her this? Of course not. Don't believe it until you've thought the whole thing through. Do a little detective work in your mind.

But, even if everyone <u>does not</u> think you're stupid, it still hurts to think your very own sister thinks you are. Even if you <u>know</u> you're not stupid, it upsets you to hear it from somebody you care about. Not only do you care about her, but you also care about what she thinks of you. In this case, the "bullied," which would be you, might knock himself out trying to please her. You might start quoting things from your school text books, trying to convince her you're smart. Or maybe, you tell her about some science show you saw on TV and what you thought of it, hoping to prove you're not what she thinks. But all this isn't necessary because she doesn't <u>really</u> think you're stupid. All that work you're going through just to impress her is only giving her more power (remember, bullies like control). She enjoys seeing you squirm; now she knows she got to you--the game worked!

It would have been much nicer for her to have said, "I'm mad that you forgot to do the dishes (no name-calling)." The proper way to handle anger is to be mad at the action <u>not</u> the person. But, unfortunately, the bully only knows how to play the game <u>her</u> way.

Bad Control

Don't confuse <u>bad</u> control with <u>good</u> control. Your parents use good control when they tell you to put a jacket on before you go outside. This is for your own good, so you don't get sick. Sound fair? Well, bad control <u>is not</u> fair. At least not to you. And the bully uses it only for <u>his</u> own good.

When a bully uses bad control, he might act bossy, sneaky or like a know-it-all. Sometimes all three. And don't ever expect to hear a "Please" or "Thank you" because the bully doesn't know these words. This person <u>has</u> to win this control game. And you may feel as if you have to let him have his own way--or he might force you to give in to him.

For example, you get a new CD for your birthday. Your parents don't want you to take it to school because they're afraid it might get lost or broken. But you want all your school buddies to see how cool it is, so you persuade them to let you take it.

Now the bully sees what you have and comes up to you outside of school. Quickly, you stuff the CD into your back-pack. "What's that you got there in your pack?" He demands.

The Bully Games

After you tell him which CD it is, he goes on and on about how that's the exact same one he's been wanting. Now he's asking you if he can borrow it. So you tell him how your parents wouldn't be cool with that. "Come on," he says, "you don't have to tell them (Bossy)." "They won't care (Know-It-All)." Now comes the "Sneaky" part--as soon as your back is turned, he reaches into your back- pack, grabs the CD and, BANG! He's off and running with it.

"I'll bring it back tomorrow, I swear!" You hear him yell as he rounds the corner with <u>your</u> property. Not only has he got your CD, he's also got control of the game (Bad Control). It was a dirty trick, but he still won. I'll tell you how to deal with this later. Just keep reading. Have you ever had something like this happen? Makes you mad, doesn't it?

The Sneak Attack

The sneak attack isn't always going to be something that's <u>done</u> to you. Sometimes, it can be something that's <u>said</u> to you. This is a great game--if you enjoy feeling like the dirt on the bottom of your sneakers. What happens is that the bully tells you something not-so-great about yourself. For example, she might say, "I don't want to hurt your feelings but, has anyone ever told you that your ears stick out?"

Now a <u>real </u>friend might talk to you about something like this if you want her advice or whatever. But, the bully will keep jabbing into you about those ears and other things--constantly. She always has to be "criticizing" you, or picking at you about something--especially when your feeling down or not in the mood. She can sense what your weak points are, and then uses them against you to attack. Mmmm... Kind of makes her a coward, doesn't it?

The part that makes this attack sneaky is the tone of voice the bully uses. She's saying something rude, but her voice sounds sweet. It's like she's pretending she really is helping you out by telling those things. Pointing out things she doesn't like in you helps to cover up how bad she feels about things in herself.

When she starts out her sentence with the words "I don't want to hurt your feelings but..." Sorry to say, she actually <u>does</u> want to hurt your feelings. But always remember not to take these comments too seriously or personally. Keep in mind that the bully probably has a lot of her own problems built up inside her. She needed someone to take it out on, and you and your ears got in the way!

Sometimes the bully might say things to keep the heat off herself. For example, she might have a big nose, squinty eyes, or chubby fingers. But if she points out your ears, it takes the attention off of <u>her</u> appearance. Nobody is perfect, but the bully couldn't stand being told she wasn't. If <u>she</u> were criticized, that would make her feel she'd lost control.

So, be extremely cautious of sentences that start out like, "Has anyone ever told you...," or "I don't want you to feel bad but..." And don't be fooled by that "I'm only telling you these things to help..." attitude. Look closely before you trust someone. If they have a soft voice but a sharp tongue--you better stop, duck and run!

The Fake

This guy will drive you bonkers by <u>telling</u> you one thing, but <u>meaning</u> something else. For example, say you have a pair of shoes that have seen their day--crusty, falling apart, hole at the toe... (you know the kind!) You just haven't gotten around to getting new ones yet. Well, the bully, seeing this great opportunity, comes up to you and says, "Oh, I <u>love</u> your shoes--I want ones just like 'em!" (Heh Heh!)

Ha Ha, very funny, you're thinking. It's best to just laugh along with this type of sarcasm. The only problem is, the bully thinks he's <u>a lot</u> funnier than what he is. Most of the time he's not even saying stuff like that to be funny. He's saying it to be mean.

If you say, "You didn't mean that...," (about loving your shoes) he'll get defensive and reply, "Geez, man, all I did was try to tell you how cool your shoes look--all beat up and everything--and now you're going off on me?"

Maybe you should've suddenly burst into a lot of fake laughter and acted like it was so funny you couldn't stop laughing, saying loudly, "<u>You are so funny</u>! I am impressed!" That might've shut him up.

In this game, the bully says nice things to you (his "victim") in a not-so-nice voice. If that confuses you, his game is working. Never try to question his tone of voice because then he'll blame you for being the not-so-nice one. (As he did with the shoes) First he's a wise guy, then he tries to blame <u>you</u> for starting something.   Surprise! This game actually works a couple different ways. Say you actually had on some new, cool-looking shoes and you ran into that same bully. He might honestly tell you that he really does love your shoes. But wait! Now he proceeds to go on about how they'll probably be out of style next year, and how he heard they're really bad for your feet. He's doing a good job of pretending he's concerned, BUT HE ISN'T!

Fakes like to throw out these double messages. He seemed nice, but somehow he got you feeling bad. Sometimes they're so-o sickening sweet, you want to gag!

TAKING THE BULLY BY THE HORNS

When this happens, pretend you're rubber and let his comments bounce right off of you. You don't need this game.

The Mind Jam

Ready to play a senseless game? Have you ever been cut off right before you got a chance to say something? The bully asks you a question (doesn't sound bad so far, huh?) and then walks away. But (and I mean But!) it's the type of question she asks you that makes this game icky.

Here's a quick example to this quickly-ending game: Let's suppose you're not doing too well in math this year. In fact, you can't stand math and it's possible you might fail the class. Your question from the bully is, "So, how's your math class coming along?" Before you get a chance to answer, she's gone. She said it in a normal tone of voice; she wasn't sounding sarcastic or anything. But the fact that she left before you could answer should tip you off. Her plan was to make you feel bad, and she didn't have to stick around to see that it worked because she knows that it worked.

The bully loves getting the last word in this game, and all you're left with is a bunch of unspoken answers jammed in your head. Should you take an aspirin and forget about it? No. Chase after her and say loudly, "Wait. I didn't answer your question. Come here and let's talk about it. I don't want to be rude and not answer you." Now you got her off guard. You can bet she wouldn't be ready for that! Plus, you got the last word. If she loses this game enough times, she might stop playing. Good for you!

The Low Blow

Again, another word game. The bully has proven to us that he's an excellent juggler of words. In this particular game, he wants you to depend on him for praise--but you don't need praise from him to feel good about yourself. Maybe he is lacking in something <u>you</u> have. He'll try to talk you out of believing you have this good quality so he can pull you down to his size. But beware of what a smooth talker he is. He'll build you way up--as high as a tree--and then chop you right down!

Example: He's afraid of the dark and you're not. First he tells you how brave you are. Then he proceeds to tell you horrible, scary things about darkness until he gets you as scared as him. Then he'll end with, "But I'm sure none of those horrible things could happen to you--since you're so brave and everything."

He planted seeds (ideas) in your brain that'll grow into giant weeds and clog your thoughts about how you <u>really</u> feel about different things. He has you convinced that everything he does or thinks is right. (As if <u>his</u> way is the <u>only</u> way!) You might forget about yourself and what <u>you</u> really think. Of course, he could care less about what you really think.

Do you want to depend on somebody else to think for you? He's controlling you, and you might become his favorite puppet. What would you do if he cut the strings?

Cut yourself free <u>now</u>. Then do a little weeding in your brain, removing all thoughts that aren't your own. You will seem more like yourself again. It's good to have you back!

You Can't Win

The last game we'll discuss is the meanest, sneakiest, and most tricky of them all. Logic won't help you to figure this one out. It's sort of a "wrong if you do, wrong if you don't" situation. First the bully puts you on the spot by giving you a choice. By making you think, she's controlling you. Next, she has you feeling trapped. But, if you take a step back and look at what's happening, you could win this game.

Say you have a friend who's a bully. (Or should that be the

other way around?) She wants you to join the basketball team with her, but you have other things going on right now. Now get ready for the ultimatum. (The ultimatum = "Do it my way, or else...") She says, "If you don't join the team with me, I won't be your friend anymore. So, what's it gonna be?"

Now she's given you your choices. Either join the team and have her friendship; or, don't join the team and lose her friendship. She has you pulling your hair out trying to solve this puzzle. What do you choose? Do you know what your decision should be? The answer is--you don't <u>have</u> to choose. Tell her, "I'm not gonna play your game anymore," meaning "You can't make me choose."

Now, throw the game back in her face. "How about this: I'm <u>not</u> going to join the basketball team, and <u>you</u> can decide if you want to be my friend or not." By <u>mirroring</u> the situation, you're throwing the game back at her and, most likely, she'll end up backing down. <u>She</u> has the choice to make now, and <u>you</u> have the control. She won't like having to play her own game.

Never let anyone threaten you. Remember that bullies can't <u>make</u> you do anything. And always keep in mind that the more power you take away from them, the less chance you'll get hurt.

Choosing <u>Not</u> to Play

Did any of those games sound familiar? The bully picks you for his opponent (without your permission) to play games that are only good (and fun) for him. Now you know that these are <u>his</u> games and <u>his</u> rules and you don't have to play. Later in this book, I'll show you how you can fight back in these unfair games.

It makes sense that there must be as many different types of bullies as there are games. One bully might specialize in only one type of bullying (game), while another might love to

The Bully Games

play all different games, so he's sure to get you one way or the other!

Remember, a bully is both sneaky and clever. There could be one playing a game in your life right now. Sometimes it takes a little time for the bad thoughts he planted in your mind to grow. And when they start to grow, boy you'll know it. If you begin feeling bad about yourself, re-read the games section of this book and see if one matches what you're going through. You can't stop the bully from trying to bully you, but you <u>can</u> stop yourself from feeling bad. In other words, <u>he</u> doesn't control you, <u>you</u> control you.

The next chapter shows you what happens to someone when they play the bully's game and lose. They become like a fly caught in a spider's web - his victim.

3
THE VICTIM

Why Me?

If you choose to stay friends with someone who's a bully, then you'll probably be saying, "why me?" a lot. But it's <u>your</u> choice. You should know that dealing with a person who bullies could cause you to feel nervous, sick, and stressed out at times. This person may try to drive you, and everyone around him, crazy so that <u>he</u> ends up looking like the normal one. (Bullies love sucking up that kind of attention.)

If you're sick, tired, or down, you can bet that the bully will try to keep you that way. And you soon find out that it's no fun waking up shaking with your bed damp from worry-sweat. Your worst nightmares may seem to become reality. You might also feel frustrated, as if a giant hand is holding you back. Like when you try to run in a dream, but you can't.

The important thing for you to do is learn to understand why he bullies you, and to <u>not</u> take it personally. So, if you think you can handle being friends with someone like that, and dealing with their "games", good for you, and good luck!

Are You "The Victim?"

In a recent Midwestern study, 76.8% of the students said they had been bullied. And 14% of those who were bullied said they experienced severe (bad) reactions to the abuse.

Discovering you're a victim isn't always obvious, or easy. You might be hanging out with somebody, and even though you consider him a friend, you feel that something isn't quite right. Something may be eating at you, but you're not sure exactly what it is. Maybe, whenever you're around him, the hair on your arms spikes out into razor-sharp needles. That's a blinding sign that this guy must really be bugging you!

Do you feel as if you're being drained of your power? Remember, a bully <u>has</u> to have you around. He <u>has</u> to control you. He <u>has</u> to overpower you. He might admit that he's been bullying you, but he would never break up the friendship. He'll act nice to get you to stay, then start up hissing and biting again later. And he secretly feels you're a fool for staying friends with him.

Sometimes bullies know they're bullying, and sometimes they don't. Either way, you still get shot down. If he doesn't know he's bullying you, it becomes <u>your</u> problem. You need to react and treat him as if he is the bully. (Because he is!) There are three things you should do:
1. Tell him what he's been doing to you and how it makes you feel.
2. Stick up for yourself. Decide you're <u>not</u> going to take it anymore.
3. If he's not willing to listen to you and understand what he's doing, stay away from him.

The Victim

He might come around if he's afraid he may lose you as a friend--that is, if he really is interested in your friendship. Most of the time bullies are only interested in your weaknesses. (Control)

If he is blind to the fact that his claws are pinching you, and pleads in his defense that he's not the bully--get ready. His next statement might be an accusation that you're actually the bully--or why else would you have called him such a thing, and made him feel so-o bad. It's senseless to argue about this with him since he obviously chose not to hear you out. This is definitely your cue to stay away.

And don't let his "hurt act" upset you. It's not your fault. You didn't cause his bad feelings. Because, first of all, he's not actually hurt, he's trying to take you on a guilt trip. Secondly, you have to think about something first in order to cause it. And you didn't plan his hurt. He planned yours.

F-E-A-R

Has anyone ever caused your heart to pound so hard that you felt as if you had a frog in your shirt trying to get out? The bully may try to scare you to get you under his control. But fear is a negative emotion, and it's also a huge waste of your time and energy. Don't let him suffocate you.

Remember the Cowardly Lion in the Wizard of OZ? Through out the entire movie, the witch kept trying to scare him. But, in the end, he realized he had the courage to face her all along. The strength to deal with her was inside himself, and all he had to do was look inside himself, find it, and use it!

Calm down, and remember you have a ton of power and strength inside yourself. Imagine it pounding through your body with a strange, tingling warmth, like electric rain. Now, you're ready to deal with this clown! (or witch!)

If saying things like, "Stop picking on me," "Go away," and

"Leave me alone," don't work--walk away. And if you have to walk a couple blocks out of your way just to avoid having your sneakers thrown in the creek, then do it! (it's worth it!)

Girls as Victims

A lot of girls feel that if no physical bullying has been done to them, then they haven't been bullied, period. However, after reading the Games' section of this book, they learn that in some cases, they were being bullied but didn't realize it.

 An awesome amount of "mind games" can go on and, unfortunately, you can end up feeling like the "victim" if you don't talk, dress, do your hair, or wear your makeup <u>their</u> way. Some may act as if they're the "Queen." But they're not your maker (or ruler). (They probably got a bug up their butt!) So, be yourself and always do what you feel inside is right. Nobody was born to play the "victim," so don't let it be you.

Of course, you might have also experienced some physical bullying from either girls or boys. Because you're a girl, you might have been chosen as the bully's victim due to the fact that girls have always been thought of as being (weaker) more emotional and less physical.

However, this isn't always the case. You can't put any one group of people into a category and say, "These people do this," or "These type of people are like that." That goes for age, gender, religion and race. Because of free will (making our own choices), and character development, we're all individually different.

The Victim

In any case, you shouldn't be considered weaker just because you're a girl. Girls can pack just as hard of a punch as boys. That means physically <u>and</u> with a sharp choice of words. So, if you're thinking of "attacking" a girl because they've been thought of as "weaker"--bullies beware.

Call Me "Victim," Please

This may sound a little creepy, but some people <u>want</u> to be victims. They put themselves down all the time. "Look how disgusting I am," etc. And they might wear sloppy clothes because they have no respect for themselves. They also might wear their hair covering part of their face--a way of hiding from their <u>cruel</u> world. It's a sad shame, really.

They might be late all the time, then cringe and hide from you, assuming you're extremely upset with them. They're trying to make you look like the bully, so they can play the victim.

Why would anyone want to do this, you're asking? Most likely because they had a bully in their past, and now the bully is stuck in their head. They actually were victims for so long, now they don't know how to stop.

Nothing is ever their fault, and they tell you bad stories about themselves, not so you pity them, but so you agree that they are worthless. They feel completely unworthy of your friendship and truly believe they are victims of life.

You can try to explain to them their misunderstandings, then suggest they talk to the guidance counselor. You also might try building up their ego, even if they seem unreachable. Make them listen. But they need to decide, on their own, that they want to stop feeling like miserable losers.

Wimp, Wuss, or Victim

It's not nice to call anybody a wimp or a wuss, but if you

allow yourself to be a victim, that's what others might refer to you as. The bully makes you feel weak so he can feel stronger. Then you start acting weak because you start believing you are. Your best defense is to ignore the bully. If you stop believing you're a victim, you'll stop being one. The mind can do amazing things. Whatever you think you are, you might become. So, be careful what you think.

The Making of a Victim

When we're first born, we're all basically the same: Little, innocent sponges soaking up everything we see and hear around us. We learn a lot simply by watching and listening to other people.

However, if we're around <u>anyone</u> who bullies us while we're growing up, we might start to close up. Meaning, we become afraid and don't want to be open to what we see and hear from those people anymore. We learned that some (or maybe only one) of them made us feel bad because we were too open, innocent, and willing to learn. Now we're not sure who we can trust anymore. We don't want to feel bad ever again, so we shut down. And by doing that, we shut out <u>everyone</u> from our lives to make sure those bullies can't get in and harm us.

Unfortunately, when we do this, we also shut out the people who really care about us. But our defense told us to protect ourselves, so we built this high, stone wall around us to keep everyone out.

People like these could remain victims all their lives because they can't forget what happened to them. Who they can or cannot trust has become blurred. What they need to know is that there is nothing wrong with them. They were right to be so open, innocent and willing to learn. However, you need to know which people to let in your life, and which

The Victim

people to shut out. And most of the time, bullies qualify as the shut-out's!

By the time you get to this section of the book, it all should start to make sense for you. Hopefully, you've learned how to spot different bullies, so you'll know who you should be careful to trust or not.

"The Victim" Plays "The Bully"

An example of how a victim becomes a bully would be the person or child who's told he's wrong all the time. Pretty soon, getting tired of the criticism, he might not be willing to be wrong anymore. It's painful, so he starts believing he is always right. Soon, <u>he</u> becomes like the bully who always told <u>him</u> he was wrong. (Bully Cycle) And if you saw him, you might guess that there was a bully in his past, simply by the fact that he talks a lot and doesn't listen.

The opposite effect of this type of bullying would result in the victim becoming shy and quiet. He becomes too afraid to say or do anything. Now he can't be told he's wrong anymore. He can't stop fearing the rejection he received.

But neither of the victims in these examples are living healthy lives. They are both living in extremes. One has become a loud-mouth know-it-all, the other, a hermit. They need to find a happy middle. If they had learned how to handle bullying, they might not have gone off the deep end. What they don't know is that they're the ones who were "OK," and the ones who were bullying them had the problem. Now, nobody is "OK", and a lot of other people will be affected by them and it will go on and on . . .

You're OK

Now don't think, because of the last section, that everyone who is quiet is a victim. Some people are naturally quiet, while others might simply choose to be quiet because it suits them. When you look closely at a person's situation, you can better understand why they act as they do.

That's why the next chapter is so important. We'll talk about how a bully becomes a bully and why they act as they do. They really do have a lot of problems. Sometimes they can be helped; but, other times they're either too far gone, or totally unwilling to listen. But no matter how they bully you, you need to know that they do it because they have a problem, not because you caused it. It's not your fault. And nobody can <u>make</u> you feel anything, unless you allow it.

Go some place where nobody can hear you and repeat out loud three times, "I'm OK." Now, believe it!

The Victim Quiz

If you're not sure if you've ever been bullied, or if you don't know whether you're a victim or not, try taking the fun quiz on the next page and see what you think!

The Victim

1. If you've ever prayed for an eclipse just to avoid seeing someone--you might be a victim.
2. If the only thing you've gotten out of a certain friendship is a sand blasting "headache"--you might be a victim.
3. If you feel the need to wear a garlic necklace before going to a party--you might be a victim.
4. If you pretend you're a Ninja fighter with imaginary enemies and call out, "Now you get yours!"--you might be a victim.
5. If someone has ever bugged you so much, you start visualizing a giant fly swatter swinging at them--you might be a victim.
6. If a certain person causes you to feel as if an evil beaver is gnawing away at your insides--you might be a victim.
7. If you would rather be in the eye of a hurricane than in the same room with someone--you might be a victim.
8. If you dream you're a lion ferociously shaking a snake between your teeth, and the snake looks familiar--you might be a victim.
9. If your breathing stops as you look directly into the eyes of a werewolf, then realize it's your friend--you might be a victim.
10. If you're considering being dropped off at school by helicopter to avoid passing someone's house--you might be a victim.

Seriously, being a victim isn't any fun and there are <u>many</u> different ways you might be bullied: Name-Calling, Physical Attacks, Sexual Abuse or "Bad Touching," Put Downs, Swearing at You, Hurting Your Feelings, Making You Self-Conscious, Crushing Your Self-Esteem, Embarrassment, Stealing/Breaking Your Stuff, Making Fun of You, Making You Cry, Controlled Confusion, Scaring You, Threats--all done to make you feel bad.

Being bullied can include something as big as being

45

physically hit or knocked down, to something as small as somebody burping in your face all the time. The first is extremely serious, while the second is extremely annoying. However, both need to be dealt with immediately.

There shouldn't have to be <u>any</u> victims in the world . . .

The next chapter talks directly to bullies. It shows more examples that will help you recognize when someone might be bullying you. But, it also might help you recognize when <u>you</u> are bullying someone else.

4
HOW A BULLY BECOMES A BULLY

Are You a Bully Too?

Since you're reading this chapter, does that mean you're a bully? Or do you know somebody who's a bully and you'd like to find out what makes her/him tick? Or maybe you're just curious and want to know what this is all about, huh?

Well, if you are a bully and you're reading this, "Bravo!" You've taken two steps toward helping yourself to stop. One, by admitting it to yourself. And two, by taking the time to read this. Thank you, and welcome!

Remember what we've talked about before: Nobody is really a "bully." It's only a costume you slip into when you feel the need to play a mean character to protect yourself. Hopefully, by the end of this chapter, you'll want to hang that costume way in the back of your closet and forget about it!

If you understand what we're learning in this chapter, then you will have the knowledge to stop bullying and start feeling better about yourself. But keep in mind that change takes time, so be <u>patient</u>. People who play "The Bully" will probably have a hard time waiting for themselves to change.

TAKING THE BULLY BY THE HORNS

Why You Act Like a Bully

You need to ask yourself some questions to find out why you bully: Did <u>anybody</u> bully you as a child? And if they did, was it anyone close to you? Maybe somebody you looked up to or trusted? Did this person try to control you, and do you remember feeling afraid? Do you feel now that this person didn't understand you? Can you think of better ways he/she might have handled things?

If you find yourself bullying, because it was done to you, you probably don't feel too hot about yourself. And if you don't respect yourself, you'll probably bully more. Maybe you can't understand why anybody would want to be your friend. Do you think that deep down inside you might feel you're unworthy of their friendship? So, you bully them because you can't respect anybody who would want to hang out with you?

Or maybe you bully everyone, whether they like you or not. All because you've become bitter from the bully-abuse you had to deal with growing up. Maybe it's a type of revenge, taking your built-up anger out on innocent people to make up for the pain others caused <u>you</u>.

Or is it possible that maybe you don't feel you do it on purpose? You learned to act like that because that's how you were treated growing up. Maybe you felt that all people acted that way and it was normal. Perhaps, you got so used to feeling bad, you just took it, not knowing <u>how</u> to feel good.

There's a lot of "maybe's" here. You need to think for yourself and find out exactly how you got to the point you're at. Why do you do the things you do? How does it make you feel? Do you think that maybe you bully so nobody can bully <u>you</u>?

Really take the time and go over examples in your head of times when you knew you weren't being nice--when you knew you hurt someone.

How Do You Stop?

Try reversing the situation. Visualize times when you hurt people emotionally and physically. Now, picture exactly what you did to them and imagine <u>them</u> doing that same thing to you. How do <u>you</u> feel being bullied by you? It's not a pretty picture, is it?

Sometimes you have to put yourself in another person's sneakers to try to understand what they're going through. Again, this is something you need to work out in your own mind. You need to go back and see if you can find that bully in <u>your</u> past. Then, decide you don't want to act like him or her. Clear out all those cobwebs of bad feelings that are stacked like giant pyramids in your mind. Start over--decide, <u>"I'm better than that."</u> Being nice to people might feel just as good as being nice to yourself.

And the next time you find yourself in a situation with someone you're itching to bully--STOP. And quickly reverse it. See yourself from their point of view. Is there another way of settling something other than you playing "The Bully?" Does bullying actually make you feel better? Would you want somebody to do that to you? Could you still like yourself when it's all over?

Of course there may be times when someone really bugs

49

you. <u>Stop</u> yourself before you go to push or strike somebody out of anger, or swear and say hurtful things to them. Bite your hand (not too hard!), and walk away. Now, who's the bigger person? You might even try to think of at least one thing you like about him or her. That will help water down some of your anger. Practice letting go of it without hurting yourself or others. Because anger, like fear, can be a negative emotion in these situations. And all it does is make you sick and gets you into trouble. You <u>are</u> better than that. (Punching your pillow always helps too!)

The Fine Line Between "Bully" & "Victim"

This section isn't about labeling somebody "Bully" or "Victim." It's how you react to, and handle situations that makes the difference.

Follow this chart of events and see if you can tell if Sam will end up as "The Victim," or "The Bully":

1. Jack bullies Sam by putting him down.
2. Sam doesn't realize Jack hurt him, yet somehow he feels bad.
3. Jack sees Sam feels bad, and realizes Sam's not gonna fight back.

How a Bully Becomes a Bully

4. Jack makes up excuses for hurting Sam, and convinces himself that anyone who doesn't stick up for themselves <u>deserves</u> to be bullied. So he keeps it up.
5. Jack loses respect for Sam because Sam won't defend himself.

Now, those of you who voted Sam would end up "The Victim" are correct. But wait, those of you who voted Sam would end up "The Bully" are also correct.

You see, there <u>is</u> a fine line between "Bully" and "Victim." Sam could go either way. Or he could become both (grey area). Sometimes, things are not simply black or white.

Let's give this story two different endings so we can see how easy it would be for Sam to play either character:

6. Jack continues to bully Sam until Sam becomes so sick from feeling bad all the time, that he decides to dive under the covers of his bed and never face anyone again.
6. Jack continues to bully Sam until Sam becomes so tired of it that he loses control. He starts treating Jack the same way Jack treated him, maybe even worse. (Bully Cycle again!)

If Sam had chosen the "Right" character, instead of the "Bully" or "Victim," it would have been better and healthier for everyone involved. For example:

6. Jack continues to bully Sam until Sam decides enough is enough and confronts Jack with the problem. If Jack listens and decides to stop what he's been doing, great. If not, Sam walks away. (Ignoring can be a great defense!)

In this case, Sam did the right thing by facing Jack. It was up to Jack's reaction to the confrontation as to how the story turned out.

TAKING THE BULLY BY THE HORNS

Bullying = No Respect

Do you remember point #5 in the previous chart of events between Jack and Sam? Jack lost respect for Sam because Sam wouldn't defend himself. Jack can't respect somebody who doesn't respect themselves. The more lack of respect Sam seemed to have for himself, the more Jack wanted to bully him.

Maybe Sam feels unworthy of anybody's respect. Possibly because he was bullied by others before Jack. So, now Sam allows himself to be bullied.

Do you know anybody who doesn't have self-respect? Do they seem as if they can't accept your friendship? Maybe they are so used to being bullied that they can't accept your affection. They probably don't feel they're good at anything either, and have a hard time accepting praise as well.

They also agree with everyone, afraid of what people might think if they were to be "themselves." They are followers. There is no middle for them. So, they become too easygoing because they're afraid of appearing unreasonable. Kind of reminds you of little kids who would buy you candy so you would be their friend. Except, in this extreme case, they'd give you all their candy and refuse the friendship, feeling unworthy of both!

This type of person is a magnet for bullies! They want to be bullied, not only because they don't think much of themselves and feel they deserve it, but also because they've felt bad for so long, they've become comfortable with feeling that way. Change scares them, and if they were to suddenly feel good, they wouldn't know what to do. Because, if they feel good, then they're open to somebody rejecting them and causing them to feel bad. But they think, if you already feel bad, you can't sink any lower, so what's the worse that could happen? Their lack of self-respect acts as a shield for them.

And the bullies love thinking that somebody might actually

have more problems than them. The weaker somebody else is, the more powerful the bully feels. Having that person for a snack might help the bully to forget about his own problems.

However, <u>we all</u> might have bullied this type of person before, no matter how many problems we may, or may not have. If you know somebody like this, do you find sometimes that they act sickening sweet? It's as if nothing makes them mad. Can you think of somebody that almost <u>asks</u> to be teased?

So, you find yourself saying or doing things (bullying!) to try to upset them, but it doesn't work. They just won't bend. They might cower a little, but they still don't release their anger.

Charlie Brown is a good example of somebody who doesn't have any self-respect, and allows others to bully him all the time. And if any Charlie Brown-type victims are reading this, stop letting people jerk you around! The last chapter will show you various ways of handling bad situations.

You need to do something for yourself now. Every morning, say out loud, "I'm special, and proud of who I am." Work on it and really feel the meaning in the words. God made you <u>equal</u> to others, no matter how different everyone acts. Give yourself time to flush away those built-up, bad feelings, and enjoy the new "you!" Life's too beautiful (and fun!) to waste it on bullies who don't appreciate it.

Once you've found your inner-strength, those bullies are history! And if they try to take it away from you, you're ready for them!

Frustration = Jealousy = Bullying

Not everyone bullies because they were bullied in the past. Sometimes bullying can be triggered by other emotions, such as frustration.

TAKING THE BULLY BY THE HORNS

For example: Jen got picked for the softball team, and her friend, Tess, didn't. Tess came down with mono and got cut from the team. Now she feels frustrated. Jen is on the team, but <u>she</u> isn't.

So, what happens next? Instead of being happy for her friend, Tess becomes jealous of Jen. Then she proceeds to go to all of the softball games and yell out rude comments. Like when she sees Jen is up to bat she might shout, "Ouuuuu, here comes the champ!" (in a smart, sarcastic tone) Or she'll make a wise-guy comment to the person next to her and say, "Huh, she's been named M.V.P. (Most Valuable Player) If I was on the team, it would have been <u>me</u>." She says these things because she's afraid Jen actually is better than her.

Tess might not have ever bullied Jen before, but being cut from the team was tough to take. And not being as tall and thin as Jen didn't help much either. Well, Tess made all those problems for herself. She needs to grow up and realize that good and bad things happen to everyone. And when something good happens to someone we care about, it's only natural, and normal, to be happy for them. Not sit around feeling sorry for yourself and yelling out sarcastic comments, hoping to take some of the other person's happiness away.

Tess wants something Jen's got. She needs to look inside <u>herself</u> and find her own good qualities. Everyone is good at something.

She also needs to learn the true value of a friend. Both

people should put the same amount of effort into the friendship (50/50). But, it's not that she doesn't want to be friends with Jen, she doesn't know <u>how</u> to be friends with Jen. And if she continues to treat everyone that same way, she might really need a friend one day, call out, and get a whole lot of "nothing" back. (Only the sound of crickets chirping)

What Happens to Bullies?

This whole time we've been discussing how bullies like/need to control. But, <u>they're</u> the ones who are really being controlled. That's right, the past events that caused their bad feelings are controlling them now, forcing them to act spiteful. A good way to stop themselves from bullying would be to destroy all those negative thoughts that keep soaring around. And, as I mentioned before, that takes time.

Take a look at the next two examples. The first example shows what might happen to the bully who decides he wants to change, and manages to clear most of those negative thoughts away.

The second example shows what might happen to the bully who doesn't want to change, or doesn't feel he needs to change and refuses to admit he's had any negative thoughts or experiences.

1. The bully hurts someone.
2. The bully admits he was wrong.
3. The bully feels sorry for it.
4. The bully tries to make up for it.
5. The bully makes mental note to try not to let it happen again.

The Opposite:

1. The bully hurts someone.
2. The bully decides that the person somehow deserved it.

3. The bully gets in a bad mood, refusing to feel guilt.
4. The bully doesn't feel he owes anyone an explanation.
5. The bully will do it again, if given the chance.

The first person is healing himself and well on his way to hanging up that bully costume, or better yet, burning it! The second person might be impossible to change. He needs to get tired of where he's at, and change on his own. He is the type you should stay away from, or avoid whenever possible. Maybe after he loses his friends he will feel lonely enough to do something about himself.

And the victim isn't the only one who can end up feeling physically and emotionally sick. The bully can also wind up depressed from all the guilt he tried so hard to hide. He may even hope you see how sick he is, pity him, and be his friend again.

But, beware of the bully who doesn't feel bad about anything he's done. You cringe when you see him coming, and you could swear he has fangs! This guy might wear a black bandanna around his leg, whir by you on his bike while spitting gum into your hair (gross!), and laugh all the while at how easy it is to get (bully) you. He may seem as if he has no emotions at all. Like if you cut him open with a knife, there would be nothing but wires!

That guy is so selfish and far into himself that he probably drove everyone in his life away from him. Because he had to have <u>his</u> way <u>all</u> the time, he flushed all his friends down the toilet in the process. There is a small percentage of bullies out there that are <u>this</u> merciless and devious. And you can be 100% sure that they need some sort of professional help! Stay far--far away from this one. He has no conscience, shows no mercy, and could grow up to be a gangster!

Now you've learned that some of the main reasons why people bully include: Because they don't feel good about themselves, somebody was mean to them, they're jealous of

How a Bully Becomes a Bully

you, or they're brats who must get their own way!

Whatever their reasons are for doing it, the last chapter presents different ways to handle those situations if you're a victim, or if you're a bully, or if you're somebody watching others play "The Victim" or "The Bully."

Let's begin!

5
WHAT CAN YOU DO ABOUT IT?

Bully Mania!

No, this isn't a riddle! This is about people who feel backed up against a wall, and don't realize they have choices. So, what can they do about it? Your mind is probably spinning like a Tasmanian Devil with questions and answers, so let's get started!

This is the chapter you have been waiting for.

If You're Being Bullied

Based on what we've discussed so far, I'm sure you've discovered whether or not you're a victim. But, there are many different ways you might be bullied. Let's set up some examples and consider some solutions:

Screams of terror pierce the frigid air as a poor boy watches his new winter coat get tossed into the trash dumpster. The bully responsible for this criminal act shows no remorse. Too dramatic? Not for the bully. He thinks he's cool practicing all his tough-guy stuff on other kids. He probably looks up to all the bad guys in the movies too.

So, what do you do? You could notify someone of authority, and help the kid get his coat back out of the trash. Also, make a mental note of whom he was and what he looked like. That way, you know who to stay clear of the next time he becomes bored and needs a thrill. And there's nothing you could say to this guy because he's probably long gone as soon as the deed is done.

Now, let's say this same guy approached you and told you to give him <u>your</u> coat, or else. So, what should you do?

A. Get mad, and watch smoke come out of your ears until you have to declare your head a "fire hazard."

B. Pretend you're an escape artist, close your eyes, and hope to disappear.
C. Face the challenge by sticking up for yourself.

The last answer, "C" would be the best way of dealing with the situation. Try handling it with humor. "Man, what do you want with this old rag?" He might agree with you (not worth it) and let it go.

But say he doesn't let it go. You start getting a bad feeling about the whole thing. You're still refusing to give up the coat, so now he starts yelling and swearing at you. You could run, if you feel you could outrun him, or else he might knock you to the ground. You also could scream "Help!" loud enough that your ears pop. You might even start crying, unless you're too scared to cry. Then, maybe he'll either pity you or feel you're too pathetic to deal with.

Now, the absolute worst thing that could happen is he takes a punch at you. If he misses, or pauses after that, quickly add, "Fighting is wrong, I think we're better than that." If he isn't interested in your statement, again, RUN!

If he catches you, you could just give up the coat for your own safety. Then go immediately to the police, your parents, his parents (if you know who they are), your teachers, whoever can help. Not only do you need to get your coat back, but this guy needs to be taken care of, or  else he's gonna go after more victims. His adulthood could lead to a lifetime of crimes which would eventually land him a permanent home in jail!

What Can You Do About It?

I wouldn't recommend it, but if somebody does start beating up on you, you need to defend yourself. If <u>nothing</u> else works, try kicking him in the shins as hard as you can. That should leave him temporarily disabled for a bit. Long enough for you to run away! (What would really make that scene amusing is if the bully fell to the ground crying and called <u>you</u> a bully!)

This guy also might be the type who tries to talk you into carrying/selling drugs for him. (This happened to a 7th grade girl I know). He'll try to bully or intimidate you into taking care of the brain-killing stuff for him. These "Carriers" make it safe for the bully, so <u>he</u> doesn't get caught.

Don't be afraid to go to school because of this. If he approaches you to help him, firmly say "I'm not interested." Then, act unconcerned with what he's doing, as if you have your own problems to deal with. That way, when you notify the principal or whoever, he won't know you're the one who got him busted.

Try not to scream out at him, "Oh my God, I can't believe you're doing that! That's illegal. You could mess yourself up or die of that. You're gonna get caught and be locked away." If you say things like that and then he gets into serious trouble, he's gonna figure it was you. And depending on how stable he is in the brain, he could go after you. (Revenge!)

The dumbest thing you could do is shout, "I'm gonna tell!" Now, you're a dead give-a-way. And that goes for any crime. For your own safety, keep it quiet, hang low, and when you get to the right people, sing like a canary!

Someone like this guy needs help before he hurts himself and others. Maybe one day, after enough counseling, when he feels better about himself and has his life back on track, he'll be thankful for whoever saved him. (You did the right thing!)

When You're Related to the Bully

This would be the "relative" bully. There's also the "boss" bully, the "teacher" bully (remember my Mrs. Perch?), the "milkman" bully--sure, why not? Anyone can do it. The list could be endless!

But, when a family member bullies, the situation becomes a bit more personal. (The embarrassing mom!) It can be just as serious as other types of bullying, but there also may be some little conflicts that go back and forth between all of you. And, no, dealing with somebody's lawnmower snoring is <u>not</u> a form of bullying. It's just something you have to put up with! (Try some ear plugs!)

The TV War example: Does anyone in your family change the channel or turn off the TV while you're watching it? When you're right in the middle of something, that can be about as irritating as a pair of underpants filled with red, fire ants! And you might've done it a few times yourself too. Come on, admit it.

The only way to solve this is to either get your own TV, or try to get interested in what the other person is watching. You also could leave the room to do something else and let your grandmother, mom, dad, brother, sister, or dog have their own way. But, you might get tired of playing connect the dots with the stars in the sky if you never get to watch what you want.

If you truly feel you're being treated unfairly, talk to them about it. People don't always realize when they're upsetting someone. Sometimes you need to ask, to find out what's going on.

What Can You Do About It?

Maybe you have an older sister or brother who picks on you all the time. And it might seem deliciously tempting to do it right back, but that would make you as bad as her/him. However, you still need to stand up for yourself and not let them get away with this. Remember, you're no less important because they're older, or bigger than you. They might even feel they're better than you, but that's only ego.

Maybe one of them tells you he loves you, but doesn't show it. As long as you know you've been showing him love, don't blame yourself. Talk to him about it. But maybe he says he doesn't want to talk about it. So stare at him until he looks at you. The worse thing that could happen is he could become defensive. "So you think you know me!" (attitude) But you do know how he's made you feel.

In the last two situations, the best you can do is talk to them. If you present your situation nicely, and not scream at them, shredding your throat, they should listen to you. And, hopefully, change their attitude. But, if they don't want to listen right now, give them time to appreciate you for whom you are. At least you know you've won their respect. It takes a lot of strength, and nerve, to approach someone with a problem you're having with them. Plus, even though they're older, look who's the more mature one now!

The Bully's Opposite

Did you know that the opposite of someone who bullies, would be somebody who is too sensitive. Could this be you? Do you get upset easily at little things? Do you take things way too seriously? Or maybe sometimes your sense of humor takes a siesta without you. (Meaning you don't always get jokes, like that one!) How would you react if your older sister told you that you weren't really related to the family, that they found you in the trash outside the hospital! First, you need to understand the reason for her saying this. Is she

63

angry with you about something and trying to get back at you, or is she simply pulling your leg? Before you blow your bully horn on her, first make sure she's modeling her bully suit. Relax and trust your feelings before you hit that panic alarm. She might just be having a little fun with you. But if she keeps it up until it's not even funny anymore, and you're not in the mood, pretend you don't have ears.

Solution Contribution

We're going to put some of the many ways you might handle bullying into categories. But first I'd like to share with you a few of the not-so-violent, and undeniably silly, real-life bully examples that actually happened:

One girl sprayed her brother in the butt with perfume because he wouldn't stop passing gas on her bed! Another girl couldn't move her head because some boy, who sat behind her in school, rolled her long hair up in his typewriter! In another case, a boy put a lamp shade on his sister's head and poked her in the face, trying to turn it on!

These may all sound funny (because they are), but you have to realize that whenever somebody feels something is being <u>done</u> to them, it's considered bullying. No matter how insignificant, or stupid it may seem.

And that could include an infinite number of things: Cutting the hair off your sister's doll, shooting birds with a bee bee gun (BOO!), ramming someone's head into the television because they said they always wanted to be on TV, asking someone with thin hair if they use Rogaine, or asking someone in a slightly wrinkled shirt if they slept in it. Stop the insanity!

Be good to each other!

What Can You Do About It?

The Confrontation

This is one of the most common and effective solutions: Tell them about it. We used it in many of the previous examples. Communication is a gift that connects you to other people. If you lose it, <u>you'll</u> feel lost. And if you want to help someone, allow them to talk before you <u>tell</u> them what their problem is. Somebody <u>might</u> admit when they are wrong, but they also must be willing to change.

And don't stress more what the person <u>did</u> to you. Stress more how it made you <u>feel</u>. That way it sounds a little less like an accusation (which would only make him madder). And don't let him argue with you about how you feel because that <u>is</u> how you feel. And you're the only one who would know that!

Also, stick to the facts. If he really is willing to listen, don't give him too much information all at once. Everyone has their gag limit. And since this guy already feels gagging about himself, don't be <u>too</u> hard on him. (however tempting that may be!) Plus if you're mean to him, you'll only be proving to him he's as bad as he thinks he is. Then he'll never change!

And sometimes the confrontation doesn't even include words. That's right, putting your hand on your hip, glaring into his eyes and tapping your foot are all signs to the bully that you know what he's up to. And if he stops bullying for a second and notices you doing any of these actions, he might demand, "What?" To which you reply, "You <u>know</u> what." To which he claims <u>not</u> to know. To which you should just tell him to get a life!

Since he was too ignorant to know (or want to know) he was bullying you, you need to use the "word" confrontation. This one needs some serious talking to. What you also could do, if he's using "word" bullying such as name-calling, putting you down, or making fun of you, is to act unaffected. You could say in a low, wise-guy voice, "Oh, I'm sure," or "You would know." But you also could say nothing. Yep. Just smile at him and do absolutely <u>nothing.</u> That will really make him wonder. (And maybe a little angry) But that's <u>his</u> problem.

Excuse Me?

If someone uses "word" bullying on you, ask them to repeat the last insult they handed you. It's hard to say something the exact same way a second time. And since you took him off guard, it probably won't sound as mean the second time around. But, if it does, say nonchalantly, "Yeah, I heard <u>that</u> before," or "That's what I thought you said." Then turn your back and stroll away.

Get Them Alone

Bullies usually like to embarrass you in front of a group of people. For them it's SHOW TIME! Sometimes they need friends to attack. (bully backups) Get them alone. They're not so tough without a crowd.

After you got your bully alone, "confront" him. You could ask him who he thinks he is. But that might provoke him into saying something smart back. You could also try telling him honestly how he made you feel. It might turn out that he's more of a show-off than a bully. But that's no excuse for how he made you feel.

If he does it again, change from "how he made you feel" to what you are going to <u>do</u> about it. Don't tell him exactly what you will do. Tell him it will be a surprise. That should stop him. If it doesn't, tell everyone else what he is doing. <u>Expose</u> him.

<u>What Can You Do About It?</u>

Keeping Your Balance

If you want to change yourself, or anyone, for the better, don't expect results in a day. Expectations=disappointment. When you expect too much and then don't get it right away, you might feel anger, blame, and even revenge.

You become drenched with unnecessary, negative emotions. And those feelings could affect others around you. People have different learning abilities and possess different levels of understanding. We all have reasons for doing the things we do, or don't do. It's OK, sometimes you need to <u>let it go</u>.

(Practice Patience!)

Some Answers to Some Questions

What do you do if somebody keeps taking your things?

If "confrontation" doesn't work, try putting your name on everything. He can't claim his mom got him that cool pen when your name is clearly on it. If that doesn't work, take it back! Maybe if the bully sees you know how to play his game, he'll stop.

If that still doesn't work, as a last resort, you could take something of his. Not as "revenge," but so that he understands how it feels to be on the other end. Now he might be ready to talk. But, if he's so bad that nothing works, give him his stuff back before it gets around school that you're a bully! (Your actions might teach him honesty and humility)

Also, keep your stuff locked up or far out of sight from his busy little fingers.

How many times does somebody have to do something to you before they qualify as a "bully?"

Anytime someone does something against your will that causes you to feel bad, qualifies them as a bully. You might bully someone only one time, but you still rented that "suit" for the day!

If it would help you, you could keep some sort of diary or journal that you write in whenever someone hurts you. It

might help you to see exactly <u>who</u> your friends are, or aren't. Plus, it's good evidence if you need to confront them on their recent or past behavior. You can tell them exactly how many times they . . .

What do you do when somebody tries to force you into drinking, smoking, or taking drugs?

First of all, <u>never</u> do

What Can You Do About It?

anything if it doesn't feel right. Give a friendly, "No." If they still persist, don't give in. Put more firmness into your voice and say, "I'm not doing that," or "I can't do that." (whatever works best for you) Then go off on your own or they'll try to get you to break down. And if that happens, not only could you end up sick, but you could get kicked out of school, arrested, and be in big trouble with your parents. Not to mention, losing the respect of some of your other friends.

And if you hear the line, "If you were my friend, you would . . ." Come back with, "I am your friend, but I'm not going to . . ." Never forget to use the strength that you have.

What are some good things to say when you first "confront" someone?

Well, that depends on the situation. For example, to the person who thinks he's right <u>all</u> the time, you could say, "I'm sure you're right about a lot of things, but in this case I really feel that I . . ."

If you have something he wants and he starts his sentence, "I wish my mom was rich enough to buy me . . ." Politely reply, "I'm sorry you don't have a . . . maybe someday . . ." Or, "You can look at/use mine if you want."

If you point out something you like about him, he might feel better in which case he might treat you better. You made him realize that there is some stuff about him that isn't nasty, and maybe, he's OK. Always talk to his "OK parts."

But if you can't find anything nice to say about him, tell him he has cool hair, or a cool jacket. Smile. Tell him you're sorry he gets so upset and ask if there's anything you can do to help. He might blow you off. In which case, leave. But he also might be glad someone heard his silent flickering cry for help. If he (or she) seems to be holding back some tears, offer a hug. We'd like to believe that no bully is <u>completely</u> bad.

TAKING THE BULLY BY THE HORNS

Also, if you feel somebody really has a problem, whether they're a bully, or victim, suggest they see the guidance counselor. Since bullying is so easy, and contagious, it's best to break the circle (Bully Cycle) before it starts again.

I'm not guaranteeing what will definitely work, or not work for you. But, you'll never know unless you give some of these solutions a try.

Always remember to trust your feelings, know when you should or shouldn't give up, and to never lose hope.

Be happy . . .

I faced the thing I feared the most,
And now it all seems clear.
I've found the strength inside of me,
And all I've lost is fear.

Bibliography

Carter, James. Nasty People. Chicago.
Contemporary Books, In. 1989.

TAKING THE BULLY BY THE HORNS

Dear Reader,

   Although I may not be able to <u>answer</u> all correspondence, I am interested in knowing how this book has affected you. I promise I will personally read your letter. You may write me at:

> Kathy Noll
> 3300 Chestnut Street
> Reading, PA 19605

or E-mail at kthynoll@aol.com

TO ORDER BOOKS BY MASTERCARD OR VISA, SEND E-MAIL TO:

sencarter@compuserve.com

Include:
Credit Card Number
Expiration Date
Book Title(s)
Number of Each Title
Total Cost of Books and Shipping Fees

*additional note

"Taking the Bully by the Horns" is a self-help book/web site dedicated to helping children and young teens deal with Bullies/Self-Esteem/Violence. Supported by Schools/Child Orgs/Parents/Doctors, we explore different ways kids are bullied, mentally and physically, how the bully becomes a bully, how the victim becomes a victim, and what can be done about it. Last year, 76.8% of students surveyed said they had been bullied. Fourteen percent experience significant trauma from the abuse. It's time to do something about it.

Bully Notes

_____

_____

_____

_____

_____

_____

_____

_____

_____

_____

_____

_____

Bully Notes

_____

_____

_____

_____

_____

_____

_____

_____

_____

_____

_____

_____

_____

Bully Notes

_____

_____

_____

_____

_____

_____

_____

_____

_____

_____

_____

_____

Bully Notes

_____

_____

_____

_____

_____

_____

_____

_____

_____

_____

_____

_____

_____